All About

The Military

Everything you need to know
before going into the
United States Armed Forces

Dr. Mia Y. Merritt

Copyright ©2013
ALL ABOUT THE MILITARY
by
Mia Y. Merritt, Ed.D

All rights reserved. No part of this book
may be reproduced in any form without permission
in writing from the author or publisher.

ISBN # 978-0-9835830-5-9
Library of Congress Cataloging
in-Publication Data

Merritt, Mia

First Printing 2013
Printed in the U.S.A.

About this book

This book was written to answer all of the questions you may have about the U.S. Armed Forces, better known as the U.S. military. If you are unsure about joining the military because you do not know all that it entails, then this book is for you. Each branch of the military is explained in great detail. The educational, medical and other benefits of joining are also outlined for you. Taking the entrance assessment known as the ASVAB, knowing the requirements for qualification into the military, becoming familiar with the Physical Training assessments, and being prepared for Basic Training are also explained in detail.

Reflection questions are listed at the end of each chapter to ensure your understanding of what you learned in that chapter. Additionally, frequently asked questions are found in the back of the book and military facts are also delineated for you. This book is extremely informative and you will take a wealth of knowledge about the military away from you upon completion of this book.

Table of Contents

CHAPTER 1 Decision Making Time 1

CHAPTER 2 Qualifications for Joining 17

CHAPTER 3 Choosing a Branch to Join 27

CHAPTER 4 How Much Money will I Make? 35

CHAPTER 5 Absent Without Leave (AWOL) 45

CHAPTER 6 Military Benefits 51

Frequently asked Questions 61

Facts about the Military 68

Chapter 1
DECISION-MAKING TIME

Now is the time that you should be thinking about what you are going to do after high school graduation. Will you go to college? If so, how will you pay for college? Will you go into the military? Do you know which branch of the military you want to join? Do you know the difference between each branch of the military? What skills do you want to learn in the military? Are there any entrance exams that must be taken? The fact that you have picked up this book means that you are considering joining the military or have a desire to know more about what the military entails. This book will answer many of the questions you have about the armed forces and will provide you with detailed information, insight and clarity about the military. Finishing high school is a great accomplishment, but it is only the beginning of your transition into adulthood. Now is the perfect time to begin thinking about what you will specifically do after high school. Great things are in store for you if you plan properly, set realistic goals, and do your research. This book is a great start, so let's get started!

Finishing high school is the first of many more accomplishments that you will achieve in life. It is the stepping stone to greater things if you prepare yourself properly. You must steadily move forward now, progressing and accomplishing goal after goal. After you graduate high school, you must plunge full speed ahead into the next phase of your life and you must know exactly what that next phase is. Focus and determination will help keep you on the right track towards goal attainment. There is a bigger life waiting for you after high school and you must go and get it. Proper preparation equates to success!

The military is not for everyone and that's okay, but unfortunately, some people find out too late that the military is not a good fit for them. If you decide to join the military, then you must understand up front that you will spend an extensive amount of time away from home. You must have that fact clear in your mind when making the decision to enlist. Do your research early so that you will know most of what to expect. Ask lots of questions of people who have actually served in the military. Make a list of the pros and cons of joining. Know exactly what you are doing because once those papers are signed, there is no backing out. If you are not absolutely, positively sure that joining the military is what you want to do, then do yourself and the military a favor and do not join, at least not until you are

100% sure that joining is what you really want to do.

Should I Join the Military?

Do you want to join the military because you want to serve your country? Perhaps it is for the educational, medical, or other benefits the military offers. Some join for the purpose of seeing the world. Whatever your reason might be, make sure that you are able to handle everything else that comes with joining the military because unlike a civilian job, you cannot just up and walk away from it because it is not what you expected or because you are frustrated and tired of people telling you what to do. In the military, there will *always* be someone over you telling you what to do, when to do it, where to go, and when to go. You will not always like it, but if there is anything the military teaches, it is respect, self-control, and discipline along with mental and physical strength, structure, and courage, which can be carried over into civilian life in a very meaningful way.

The President of the United States is the Commander and Chief of the American Military, and after you join, you take a solemn oath to *"obey the orders of the President of the United States and the lawful orders of those appointed over you."* Disobeying those orders can cause serious consequences and/or penalties. If you cannot live with this actuality, then save yourself and the government some valuable time and money, and do not enlist.

The ASVAB

If you are serious about joining the military, then you must get serious about *The Armed Services Vocational Aptitude Battery* commonly known as the "ASVAB." This is a multiple test aptitude battery that helps you to identify your particular skill or talent areas. The ASVAB is the most widely used aptitude test in the world and is used by all five branches of the United States Armed Services. This battery determines eligibility for enlistment and qualification of career opportunities. The ASVAB measures strengths, weaknesses and the potential for future career success. It is only administered in English and is broken down into four areas: Arithmetic Reasoning, Word Knowledge, Paragraph Comprehension and Mathematics Knowledge. As stated, the score you get on this test will determine the type of job you will train for in the military. The higher your scores are, the better your chances are of selecting from a wider variety of jobs.

The ASVAB is administered at over 14,000 schools and Military Entrance Processing Stations (MEPS) nationwide. The Department of Defense developed and maintains this assessment piece. You want to earn as high of a score as possible, regardless of what people tell you. There are ASVAB practice booklets that you can obtain and study from so that you will know what to expect and can be well-prepared for what is on it. The practice booklets will help you identify your areas of improvement. The Armed Forces Qualification Test (AFQT) Score is the score you get after taking the ASVAB. This score determines if you "qualify" to join the military. You receive a percentile score which is valid for two years.

What if I Fail the ASVAB?

The military does not actually use the word "fail" as it pertains to the ASVAB. In fact, they tell you that you cannot actually "fail" it. However they may dress it up, the fact remains that if you "fail" to get a high enough score, you will NOT be able to enlist in the U.S. Armed Services. Not having a high score means that your AFQT score was too low. The AFQT score determines whether you are qualified to enlist in the U.S. military and your score indicates your potential for training in military occupations. If you barely meet the qualifying test score, then rest assured that you will not have a large variety of jobs from which to choose. If you score too low, you will not qualify to join the military at all. You must do your absolute best on the ASVAB so that your AFQT scores will be an accurate depiction of what you know and what your abilities are. Do the best you can so that you will be eligible for the military skill specialty that matches your ability and interests.

The AFQT score is based on population norms for males and females ages 18 to 23. In other words, your score reflects your abilities compared to males and females in your age range and gender group. This test can be taken as early as tenth grade, but those scores cannot be used to join the military because you must be a junior or senior in order for your scores to be valid for entrance. It can be beneficial for you to take it in tenth grade just to see what is on it and to see how you score. If you take the ASVAB in high school, that does not mean that you have committed yourself to joining the military. However, military recruiters may contact you after you take the test. The ASVAB can assist in identifying your interests and skills even if you are not planning to enter the military or may be undecided. Taking the ASVAB can also help you choose courses for college and make your personal career decisions.

It is important that you are very careful when answering personal information on the ASVAB. Your scores will not be accurate if any of your personal information is wrong. For instance, if you make a mistake and shade in female if you are male, then your scores will be invalid because the gender is wrong. Remember that you are being compared to your age group and gender. If you take the test in high school as a junior but mistakenly put senior on your answer sheet, your scores will be lower because you are being compared to seniors, not juniors.

Retakes

Initially, if you do not meet the minimum score for entry into the armed forces, you can retake the ASVAB, but you must first wait thirty days after taking it the first time, thirty days after taking it the second time, and six months after that. There is no limit to how many times you can take the test prior to passing, but once you meet that minimum score, you cannot retake it again. It is very important to understand that if you take the ASVAB for the first time, then a second time, it is the second score that counts - even if the second score is lower than the first score. The new score replaces the old because it is the latest test score that is considered valid. The rules for retaking the ASVAB are different for each branch of the military. If you are not enrolled in the military, your ASVAB score is valid for only two years, then it expires. After joining the military, your scores remain valid as long as you are enlisted. While you are in, you can use your scores to qualify for retraining later on.

Most branches will only allow you to retest if your previous test has expired or you failed to achieve a high enough score to qualify for enlistment. Isolated occurrences may also allow you to retake the test, such as you being called away on an emergency while taking the test, a fire drill happened or an evacuation led to the test being interrupted. Other than legitimate situations such as those, a recruiter is not allowed to have you retake the test simply for hopes of you making a higher score.

For Coast Guard enlistments, you must wait six months before you can retest for the purpose of raising scores to qualify for a particular enlistment option. The Coast Guard Recruiting Center may authorize retesting after 30 days have passed from an initial ASVAB test if a legitimate reason exists to believe the initial AFQT score or subtest scores do not reflect an applicant's education, training or experience.

The ASVAB consists of eight subject areas, known as sub-tests:

Sub-test Title	Sub-test Description	Nbr of Quest	Time
General Science	Measures knowledge of the physical and biological sciences	11	25
Arithmetic Reasoning	Measures ability to solve arithmetic word problems	36	30
Word Knowledge	Measures ability to select the correct meaning of words presented in context and to identify the best synonym for a given word	11	35
Paragraph Comprehension	Measures ability to obtain information from written passages	13	15
Mathematics Knowledge	Measures knowledge of general mathematics principles, including algebra and geometry	24	25
Electronics Information	Measures knowledge of electricity, radio principles, and electronics.	9	20
Auto and Shop Information	Measures knowledge of automotive maintenance and wood and metal shop practices	11	25
Mechanical Comprehension	Measures knowledge of mechanical and physical principals and ability to visualize how illustrated objects work	19	25

Once you become an enlisted member of the Armed Forces, you become the backbone of the military. As an enlisted member, you will perform the primary jobs that need to be done and you will be called a "Specialist" because you will be trained to perform particular "specialties" while in the military.

Enlisted Ranks

There are nine enlisted ranks in the military and as you progress up those ranks, you assume more responsibility and provide direct supervision to those under you. Enlisted personnel in certain grades have special status. In the Army, Air Force and Marine Corps, this status is known as Noncommissioned Officer status, or NCO. In the Navy and Coast Guard, such enlisted are known as Petty Officers. In the Marine Corps, NCO status begins at the grade of E-4 (Corporal). In the Army and Air Force, enlisted personnel in the grades of E-5 through E-9 are NCOs. However, some Army E-4s are laterally promoted to Corporal, and are considered NCOs. Also in the Army and Air Force, personnel in the grades of E-7 to E-9 are known as Senior NCOs. In the Marine Corps, those in the grades of E-6 through E-9 are known as Staff NCOs. In the Navy/Coast Guard, petty officers are those in the grades of E-4 through E-9. Those in the grades of E-7 to E-9 are known as Chief Petty Officers.

Physical Requirements

Much of what you are going to experience in basic training can be practiced at home before you even go off to basic training. When going into the military, it is to your extreme advantage to prepare yourself to be rigorously challenged mentally and physically. Start thinking and acting liking a soldier before even leaving your home. Potential service members must be in good physical condition, of appropriate weight and able to pass a standard physical screening prior to entry. Regardless of what branch you decide to join, you will take a Physical Screening Test (PST) after being accepted and you must pass each test. Each service branch has a different series of physical requirements, but the most common among each branch are the sit-ups, push-ups, pull-ups, endurance run and swim. If you fail the physical aspect of basic training, drill sergeants will work with you, and you will be retested after about 90 days; but if you fail a second time, then your chances of moving forward in the military are over. The paperwork is begun to have you dismissed from the military. Once it is decided that you are not ready and will not be able to pass the physical training, then you will be administratively separated or recycled through basic training. For this reason, you must stay in shape and train yourself prior to leaving so that the strain will not be so bad on you while in physical training. Below are some suggestions of what to do to prepare for physical training in the United States Armed Forces:

Stretch. Try to stretch every day so that your muscles will have increased range of motion and you will have enhanced workout effects.

Improve your push-ups. Based on how physically fit you are right now, that will determine how many push-ups you can do in a set. Push-ups enhance upper body strength. It is also important to know how to do a push-up properly:

1. When doing push-ups, make sure you are on a flat surface and your stomach is facing the floor. The arms, legs, back, and buttocks are straight and do not sag.

2. Bend your elbows to lower your entire body until your arms, shoulders and back are aligned.

3. Push your body weight back up until your arms are straight.

If this way is too challenging for you at first, then start off by doing the push-ups on a chair with your arms on the seat. Always set a goal, and after you have set your goal, challenge yourself to exceed that goal. Ideally, you should be doing

200-500 push-ups a day with at least 20-60 in a set.

Improve your sit-ups.

1. Sit-ups will enhance your abdominal strength. Having a strong abdominal area is essential to all exercises.

2. To do a proper sit-up, lay on a flat surface with your knees bent, and feet 12-18 inches from your buttocks.

3. Your arms should be crossed and your thumbs at your throat.

4. Lift your arms up then down and propel yourself forward. Your elbows should be hit 1-3 inches below your knee cap when you come up, and then lay back with your arms back into the air.

5. Your thumbs never leave your throat. If you cannot complete ten sit-ups or more in one set, then do crunches instead.

6. A crunch is the same as a sit-up, but only your back and shoulders leave the floor and your elbows never touch your knee cap. Your daily goal for sit-ups should be between 300-800 a day. Your set goal

should be 30-80 in one set, but remember to always push yourself.

Work on your pull-ups.
Pull-ups strengthen your overall upper body strength, including the arms, chest, and back. Pull-ups are difficult, and if you are not used to doing them, it will be a challenge. Pull-ups should be done on a pull-up bar or a sturdy bar that is able to support your weight. Your hands should not be much farther than shoulder width, and palms should be facing away from you.

If it is a short bar, then bend your knees and cross your legs so you support all of your weight. Pull your weight up. Your chin must reach above the bar then all the way down until your arms are straight. If you cannot complete 1-3 pull-ups then use resistance bands that are hooked from the bar to your feet so you carry less weight. Your daily goal should be 50-200 pull-ups a day, and your set goal should be 5-10 a set.

Endurance Run. The endurance run is a measure of your body's overall ability to run constantly for a period of time. The PST runs vary from 1.25 miles up to 2 miles and they are timed. In preparation for this, you should run for at least 40 minutes a day. Of course, the longer you run, the better. It is good to sprint short distances. If you cannot run for 40 minutes without stopping, then pace yourself to run as long as you can, then walk briskly for a short period as a small break. Your goal should be to run 1.5 miles under 11 minutes or less.

Swim. Not all branches have the timed swim, but for those that do, the timed swims vary from 300-800 yards in under 12-11 minutes. In preparation for this training, it would be good for you to swim for at least 30 minutes. Your goal should be to swim 40-50 second short lanes and 60-65 long lanes using the breast or side stroke, and swim 30-40 second short lanes and 40-50 long lanes using a freestyle stroke. Try to swim at least 3-7 days a week.

Applying these exercises into your daily routine prior to going into the military will significantly increase your chances of passing the physical training and will make it less demanding on your body because your body will be used to it. When preparing for your Physical Training before leaving for the military, always remember the following tips:

- ✓ Exercise daily
- ✓ Always challenge yourself.
- ✓ Exercise at least six days a week.
- ✓ Be consistent
- ✓ Be persistent
- ✓ Be focused

Reflection Questions

1) Do you know exactly what you want to do when you graduate high school? If so, explain in detail what that is using a description, what is needed to get started, time frame to start and time frame to finish.

2) If you are seriously considering joining the military, explain your reasons for wanting to join. If not the military, explain what you will do after high school and the reasons for making that decision.

3) What have you learned about the ASVAB and how your score affects you in the military?

4) Who is the Commander and Chief of the United States Military?

5) How many enlisted ranks are there in the military? Describe them.

6) Why is it important to be physically fit when going into the military?

7) What are the five most common exercises used for physical training purposes? Briefly describe each one.

8) What happens if you do not pass the physical training component the first time?

9) What happens if you do not pass the physical training component the second time?

10) What are some tips for keeping your exercise regiment strong and consistent?

Chapter 2
QUALIFICATIONS FOR JOINING
THE MILITARY

In order to become an enlisted member of the United States Armed Forces, you must have at least a high school diploma, although GEDs are accepted on an isolated basis. A majority of enlisted members in the military today already have some college background. Many have Associates and Bachelor Degrees. Some even have higher-level degrees, such as Masters and Doctorates Degrees, but just know that if you have a high school diploma, you have met one criterion. In addition to the high school diploma, each applicant must meet strict moral character standards. After your initial screening by the recruiter, an interview is conducted at the Military Entrance Processing Station (MEPS). This is an interview where you are asked lots of questions regarding your background. A credit check and/or a criminal background check is also conducted. If you have any type of criminal activity on your record, it must be explained and reviewed by military personnel. Some types of criminal activity will automatically disqualify a person from entering the military. Other cases may require a waiver, which means that the military will examine the circumstances surrounding the incident and then make a determination for qualification. Moreover, if you have a lot of debt, this may disqualify you from joining the military because applicants with large amounts of debt are not likely to overcome it on junior enlisted pay. This is why credit checks may be considered as part of the enlistment decision as well. Legal and financial situations in your past can be wavered, but you must let your recruiter know about them. There is no penalty for revealing your past problems with your recruiter. Things are always kept confidential. You cannot hold back information or lie to get into the military. When you do that, your character comes into question. Keep in mind that they look for good moral character in the military. Here is what the military has to say about moral standards of enlistment:

*Persons entering the Armed Forces should be of **good moral character**. The underlying purpose of moral character enlistment standards is to minimize entrance of persons who are likely to become disciplinary cases or security risks or who disrupt good order, morale, and discipline. Moral standards of acceptability for service are designed to disqualify the following kinds of persons:*

- Individuals under any form of judicial restraint (bond, probation, imprisonment, or parole)

- Those with significant criminal records

- Persons convicted of felonies may request a waiver to permit their enlistment. (The waiver procedure is not automatic and approval is based on each individual case.) One of the considerations in determining whether a waiver will be granted is the individual's ability to adjust successfully to civilian life for a period of time following his or her release from judicial control.

- In processing waiver requests, the Military Services shall require information about the "who, what, when, where, and why" of the offense in question; and a number of letters of recommendation attesting to the applicant's character or suitability for enlistment may be requested. Such letters must be from responsible community leaders such as school officials, ministers, and law enforcement officials.

Medical Conditions

In addition to questionable moral character, there are other things that will disqualify you from joining the United States Armed Forces, such as certain medical conditions. The Department of Defense (DOD) has medical standards that thoroughly outline which medical conditions are acceptable for entrance into the military and which are not accepted. The purpose of DOD medical standards is to ensure that medically qualified personnel accepted into the armed forces of the United States are:

1) Free of contagious diseases that would likely endanger the health of other personnel.

2) Free of medical conditions or physical defects that would require excessive time lost from duty for necessary treatment or hospitalization or would likely result in separation from the Army for medical unfitness.

3) Medically capable of satisfactorily completing required training.

4) Medically adaptable to the military environment without the necessity of geographical area limitations.

5) Medically capable of performing duties without aggravation of existing physical defects or medical conditions.

For this reason, it is of extreme importance that you divulge your medical history to your recruiter. The information is confidential, but can save a lot of time, money and embarrassment later on resulting from your failure to reveal this information.

Delayed Entry Program

The Delayed Entry Program (also called the Delayed Enlistment Program), is a program for those who plan on going into the armed services, but do not leave right away. They specify a future reporting date for entry on active duty and this date is stipulated on their contract. They go into D.E.P. before shipping out to Basic Training. The D.E.P is a contractual agreement between the recruit and their respective branch of military. This contract stipulates that they report to training on a specific date. However, if a person decides that the military is not for them, there are ways to separate from D.E.P.

While recruits are in the D.E.P., they usually spend a significant amount of time at their local recruiting office with their recruiter who will begin training them in military basics such as drill and ceremony, first aid, chain of command, and rank structure prior to leaving for training and active duty service. The time a recruit spends in D.E.P. does count towards their eight year commitment/obligated service, and specifically the reserve portion of that service. For example, if a person spends six months in D.E.P., upon entering active duty service, their contract would only be four years active and three and a half years inactive reserve. If a person decides that they no longer want to go into the armed forces, they do not have to go. They can remove themselves from the program, but their time in the Air Force Delayed Entry Program ends once they report for basic training. A recruiter will not tell you this, nor will they make it easy for you to do, but you can renegotiate your contract at any time while you are in the program. You are also not subject to the Uniform Code of Military Justice while you are in the Delayed Entry Program. You do not have to abide by military law until you actually leave for basic training.

Lying to Get Into the Military

It is *extremely* important that you are truthful with your recruiter about every relevant piece of information. It is also imperative that you not allow a recruiter to encourage, advise, or even hint that you lie about any important information. It is a criminal offense (a felony) to give false or misleading information or withhold required information on any military recruiting documentation. This offense is punishable by a $10,000 fine and/or three years in prison! This offense falls under the Uniform Code of Military Justice (UCMJ), which is the catalyst upon which military laws are based. Articles 77 through 134 of the UCMJ are known as the "punitive articles", which means that if certain offenses falling within the confines of these articles are broken, it can result in punishment by court-martial. If you get away with lying long enough to actually enlist, and are caught later, it becomes a military offense and you can be prosecuted for a violation of *Article 83* of the *Uniform Code of Military Justice (UCMJ)*, which states:

"Any person who--
1. procures his own enlistment or appointment in the armed forces by
knowingly false representation or deliberate concealment as to his qualifications for that enlistment or appointment and receives pay or allowances thereunder; or

2. procures his own separation from the armed forces by knowingly false
representation or deliberate concealment as to his eligibility for that separation; shall be punished as a court-martial may direct."

When you break a military law, you are considered to be "courts marital" and your offense is subject to the procedures and guidelines of the *Manual for Courts Martial.* Courts-martial in the United States are criminal trials administered by the U.S. Military. Their purpose is to try members of the U.S. Military for violations of the Uniform Code of Military Justice (or UCMJ), which is the U.S. military's criminal code.

The *Manual for Courts Martial* (MCM) explains the maximum punishment for a violation. Punishments may include things such as dishonorable discharge, reduction to the lowest enlisted rank, forfeiture of all pay and allowances, and confinement at hard labor for two years. The Enlistment Contract, which is DD Form 4/1, makes this very plain. Paragraph 13a of the contract signed by the recruit states:

13a. My acceptance for enlistment is based on the information I have given in my application for enlistment. If any of that information is false or incorrect, this enlistment may be voided or terminated administratively by the Government, or I may be tried by Federal, civilian, or military court, and, if found guilty, may be punished.

Each of the military services have recruiting regulations which makes it a crime for recruiters to lie, cheat, or knowingly process applicants that they know are not eligible for enlistment. Recruiters are punished when they are caught violating the standards. However, the key phrase is "when" they are caught. It should be reiterated though, that most recruiters are honest. Most importantly, you make sure that you are going in with all honesty and that any questionable past issues have been revealed. This will eliminate any problems for you down the line and you won't have to constantly worry about whether or not your dishonest secret will be found out. Honesty is always the best policy!

Reflection Questions

1) When you discover that you are qualified to join the military, what happens after your initial screening by a recruiter?

2) If you have a whole lot of debt, can you still join the U.S. military? Explain your answer.

3) What happens if you lie to get into the military and then you are found out later?

4) What is the *Uniform Code of Military Justice (UCMJ)?*

5) What is The *Manual for Courts Martial* (MCM)?

6) What are some things that can disqualify someone from joining the military?

7) What does it mean to be Courts Martialed?

8) What is the purpose of DOD medical standards?

9) What happens to recruiters that are caught violating their recruiting standards?

Chapter 3
CHOOSING A BRANCH TO JOIN

If you are seriously considering the military, you will need to decide which branch is the better fit for you based upon your interests, skills, and abilities. Each of the services are different, and some people may be more suited for one branch over another. Be sure that you select a branch that you are interested in joining based upon *your* interests and not because of someone else's interests. Just because someone in your family served in a particular branch, does not mean that you absolutely must join that branch as well. Remember, this is *your* life and you are the one responsible for your happiness and fulfillment.

There are five branches of the military: The **Army**, **Navy**, **Air Force**, **Marine Corps**, and **Coast Guard**. It has been commonly said that the Marines are without argument, the most *"military"* of all the services. The Army is said to be the second most "military". If you desire a little more flexibility in your lifestyle, but still want a strong sense of being in the military, the

Army may be for you. If you like to travel a lot, the Navy may be the best fit. The Navy also has what is called the Navy SEALS (Sea, Air, Land), which is one of the best-known special operations forces there is. If you are interested in becoming a shooter, the Marine Corps may be the branch for you. The Coast Guard only has 23 enlisted jobs to choose from (as of this writing), and you probably will not get a "guaranteed" job at the time of enlistment if you decide to go into this branch. On the plus side however, most of the jobs in the Coast Guard directly relate to the civilian job market. With not so many jobs to choose from, the Coast Guard does not "specialize" in certain areas as much as the other services do; so be mindful of this when considering the Coast Guard. Of all the services, the Air Force (tied to the Coast Guard) is probably more similar to having a regular job, but it is by far, the hardest branch to get into in terms of educational requirements and entry tests.

The Five Branches of the Military

ARMY. The United States Army is the oldest and largest U.S. Military Service. The Army was officially established by the Continental Congress on June 14, 1775 and is the main ground force of the military. There are approximately 76,000 officers and 401,000 enlisted members on active duty (as of this writing). The Army is the agency that organizes and trains soldiers for land warfare. Their main function is to protect and defend the United States by way of ground troops, armor tanks, artillery, attack helicopters, tactical nuclear weapons, etc.

The Army is supported by two Reserve Forces, which can be tapped into for trained personnel and equipment during times of need: The Army Reserves and the Army National Guard. The primary difference between the two is that the Reserves are owned and managed by the federal government and the National Guard is "owned" by each state. However, the President of the United States or the Secretary of Defense can activate National Guard members into federal military service during times of need.

NAVY. Similar to the Army, the Navy was officially established by the Continental Congress in 1775. The Navy's primary mission is to maintain "freedom of the seas." The Navy makes it possible for the United States to use the seas where and when our national interests require it. In times of conflict, the Navy helps to supplement Air Force air power. An aircraft carrier usually carries about 80 aircraft. Most of these are fighters or fighter-bombers. Additionally, Navy ships can attack land targets with very heavy guns and cruise missiles from miles away. Navy submarines (fast attack and ballistic missile subs) allow stealth attacks on the enemies from right off their shores. The Navy is also responsible for transporting Marines to areas of conflict. The active duty Navy has about 54,000 officers, and 324,000 enlisted personnel (as of this writing) and is supported in times of need by the Naval Reserves. However, unlike the Army and Air Force, there is no Naval National Guard (although a few states have established "Naval Militias").

AIRFORCE. The Air Force is the youngest military service, created under the National Security Act of 1947. Prior to that year, the Air Force was a separate Corps of the Army. The primary mission of the Army Air Corps was to support Army ground forces. However World War II proved that air power had much more potential than simply supporting ground troops, so the Air Force was established as a separate service. The primary mission of the Air Force is to defend the United States and its interests through utilization of air and space. To accomplish this mission, the Air Force operates fighter aircraft, tanker aircraft, light and heavy bomber aircraft, transport aircraft, and helicopters (which are used mainly for rescue of downed-aircrew and special operations missions). The Air Force is also responsible for all military satellites and controls all of the nation's strategic nuclear ballistic missiles.

There are about 69,000 commissioned officers on active duty in the Air Force, and about 288,000 enlisted members (as of this writing). Like the Army, the active duty Air Force is supplemented by the Air Force Reserves and the Air National Guard.

MARINE CORPS. Unlike the other branches, the Marines do not mix men and women in basic training, which upsets some people because they feel that it shortchanges women. Each gender trains the same way, but physical requirements for women are less demanding than that of men. With the exception of the Coast Guard, the Marines are also the smallest service. There are approximately 18,000 officers and 153,000 enlisted personnel on active duty (as of this writing). The Marines were officially established in November of 1775 by the Continental Congress to act as a landing force for the United States Navy. In 1798, however, Congress established the Marine Corps as a separate service. The primary duty of the Marines is to assault, capture, and control "beach heads," which then provide a route to attack the enemy from almost any direction. The Marines are often referred to as the *"Infantry of the Navy."* The Marines are generally a lighter force when compared to the Army, so they can generally be deployed fast. For combat operations, the Marines prefer to be as self-sufficient as possible, so they also have their own air power, consisting primarily of fighter and fighter/bomber aircraft and attack helicopters.

The Marines use the Navy for much of their logistical and administrative support. For example, there are no doctors, nurses, or enlisted medics in the Marine Corps. Even medics that accompany the Marines into combat are specially-trained Navy medics. Like the Navy, there is no Marine Corps National Guard, but Marines are supported in times of need by the Marine Corps Reserves.

COAST GUARD. During times of peace, the Coast Guard is primarily concerned with law enforcement, boating safety, sea rescue, and illegal immigration control. However, the President of the United States can transfer part or all of the Coast Guard to the Department of the Navy in times of conflict. The Coast Guard consists of ships, boats, aircraft and shore stations that conduct a variety of missions. The Coast Guard is the smallest military service, with about 7,000 officers and 29,000 enlisted on active duty (as of this writing). The Coast Guard is also supported by the Coast Guard Reserves and a volunteer "Coast Guard Auxiliary" in times of need.

The United States Coast Guard was originally established as the Revenue Cutter

Service in 1790. In 1915, it was reformed as the United States Coast Guard under the Treasury Department. In 1967, the Coast Guard was transferred to the Department of Transportation. Legislation that was passed in 2002 transferred the Coast Guard to the Department of Homeland Security.

NATIONAL GUARD AND RESERVES

All of the services have a reserve component but only the Army and Air Force have a National Guard. The primary purpose of the Reserves and National Guard is to provide a reserve force to supplement the active duty forces when needed. As mentioned, the biggest difference between the Reserves and the National Guard is that the Reserves belong to the Federal Government, while the National Guard belongs to the individual state's government. Both the Reserves and the National Guard can be called to active duty by the Federal Government, under the directive of the President. State governors can also call out their National Guard units to assist in state emergencies.

Reflection Questions
1) How many branches are there in the military? Name them.

2) Which branch of the service is considered the most "military"? What is considered to be the second most "military?"

3) Which branch(es) of the military has both a Federal Reserve and the National Guard?

4) What is the difference between the Federal Reserve and the National Guard?

5) Which service branch is often referred to as the *"Infantry of the Navy?"* Explain.

6) Which branch is the main ground force of the military?

7) If you are interested in becoming a shooter, which branch should you consider?

8) Which branch of the military defends the United States and its interests through utilization of air and space?

9) In 2002, the Coast Guard was transferred to which U.S. Department?

Chapter 4

HOW MUCH MONEY WILL I MAKE IN THE MILITARY?

While training and serving, you will earn a salary comparable to that of civilians so that you may continue being self-sufficient and able to pay your bills and/or care for your family. Basic pay is set by the Federal Government in order to align with civilian pay rates in the U.S. economy. Your military pay will be based upon your rank and time in service. This pertains to all branches of the Armed Forces. You will receive regular cost-of-living salary increases and raises in conjunction with promotions. Housing, uniform allowances, tax breaks and other benefits comprise the total compensation package of a serviceman/woman. In the military, you do not have to pay for food or shelter. For more detailed information on your pay, you should talk a recruiter.

Retirement

Once you have served 20 years of active-duty in the military, you will receive retirement benefits and pension, which enables you to retire at an earlier age than most civilians. Many retired soldiers enjoy full civilian careers after service, knowing they have the added financial security of a military pension. You can retire at any age and receive benefits at that time, but the amount of pay that you receive depends upon the number of years served and whether or not you retire with a disability. For instance, a soldier who served in the military for 20 years receives half the amount of their base army wage. If you retired after 30 years of service, you receive 75 percent of your base wage as opposed to 50% for 20 years of service. Over the years, pension payments can also receive cost of living adjustments.

What the Recruiter Never Told You

The recruiter's job is to find enough qualified volunteers to fill vacancies for the fiscal year for their branch of service. While a majority of military recruiters are hard-working, honest, and dedicated, there are some who are sometimes tempted to bend the truth and/or downright lie, and/or blatantly cheat in order to sign up a recruit. Some recruiters do this because of the way the recruiting system is set up. It is a numbers game pure and simple. Recruiters are evaluated based upon the number of recruits they sign up. If they sign up large numbers, they are considered to be a top notch recruiter. If they fail to sign up the minimum number assigned to them (known as "making mission"), they may find their career in jeopardy. This pressures *some* recruiters to apply unethical practices in order to "make mission." It is up to you to ask point blank, specific, no-nonsense questions and expect direct and honest answers from the recruiter. Be very suspicious of any unclear or vague answers. Always press for specifics. If in doubt, ask the recruiter to put the information in writing. You can also ask the recruiter to back up what they are saying via policy manuals, guides or pamphlets.

Basic Training

Basic Training or Military "Boot Camp" is six to thirteen weeks of extremely intense physical training and teaches war-fighting skills. However, the severe routines and control over every aspect of your life while in boot camp is several times worse than your ordinary military duties will be. This is done deliberately. It is the job of the Training Instructors (TIs) and Drill Instructors (DIs) to either alter your mind-set to a military way of thinking or weed you out before the military spends too much money on your training. This is done by applying extreme degrees of physical and mental strain while simultaneously teaching you the essentials of military rules, policies, protocol, and the logistics of your particular branch of service.

While it may seem brutal to those who are going through it, the T.I.'s and D.I.'s really do not get pleasure in your pain and anguish. In fact, after you graduate from basic training, you will find that most of them are pretty decent people. The training programs are strategically and psychologically designed to tear apart the civilian mind-set and build from scratch a proud, physically fit, and dedicated member of the United States Military. It would be very wise to go into the military with a little fore-knowledge, the right attitude, and a few survival tips, so that you can graduate basic training with minimal to no problems. You will discover that while in boot camp, it gets a little bit easier each day. The bottom line is that you enter boot camp as a civilian, but you graduate as a true soldier. Unfortunately, many people simply cannot endure the psychological and/or physical challenges involved in basic training and do everything in their power to return to the freedom, privacy and comfort of civilian life.

Before you sign the contract and take that oath, you need to know beyond a shadow of a doubt that joining the military is what you really want to do because once you are in, it is not easy getting out right away. Being in the military is nothing like having a civilian job. You cannot just up and quit because you do not like it. Sadly, a significant number of individuals who join the military do not even make it through basic training, and some of those who do make it through boot camp do not make it through their first four years. For many, the military is not what they thought it would be and they desperately want out. They entered with a false sense of what the military is all about. Most times, this is because the recruiter did a great job of selling the Armed Forces as this great occupation while magnifying the benefits, but leaving out many other important aspects of it. Family members can also add pressure to someone whose heart was not really set on the military. This only sets people up for failure many times. This is why you must learn as much as possible about the military prior to going in.

In the military, there will *always* be someone telling you what to do, when to do it, and how to do it. Failing to do what you are told can land you in jail. Joining the military is very serious and is designed for the strong in mind, body and spirit. It is designed for those with unmitigated gall and intestinal fortitude. Sixty percent of individuals who join the military actually make it to the end of their service commitment and either reenlist or walk away content with their Honorable Discharge.

After Basic Training (Boot Camp)

Depending on the service you have chosen, you will go from boot camp to Advanced Individual Training (Army), Technical Training (Air Force), Military Occupational Specialty Training (Marines), or "A" School for rate training (Navy and Coast Guard) to learn the specialized skills needed to perform your job. After your training, you will be sent out to the field fully equipped and highly skilled to do your part to keep our country safe and free. You will also have learned valuable skills that will get you far in the military as well as in the civilian world.

After basic training is over, you will go into Advanced Individual Training (AIT), where you will receive training for your Military Occupational Specialty (MOS), Air Force Specialty Codes (AFSC) or rate. A job in the Army and the Marine Corps is called an MOS. In the Air Force, the jobs are called Air Force Specialty Codes (AFSC). In the Navy and Coast Guard, the jobs are called Ratings or "rate" for short.

Some AITs are combined with basic training and are called One Station Unit Training (OSUT). This means that your Basic Training and AIT training are conducted on the same post with the same set of drill sergeants. After successfully completing basic training, you will be transformed, both physically and mentally, into a fundamental part of the United States

Armed Forces. Then, and only then, are you awarded the title of Soldier, Sailor, Airman, or Marine.

Basic Housing Allowance

A person assigned to permanent duty within the 50 states, who is not furnished with government housing, is eligible for a Basic Allowance for Housing (BAH), based their rank, dependency status, and permanent duty station zip code. If you are stationed overseas (except in Hawaii and Alaska), including U.S. territories, you are eligible for an Overseas Housing Allowance (OHA) based on your dependency status. Basic Housing Allowance distinguishes between with-dependent and without-dependent, the with-dependent compensation is based on comparable civilians using average family size. BAH amounts are set at the median for each grade and housing profile. An out-of-pocket expense may be incurred based on the actual housing of choice. If you rent above the median rate for the grade/profile, then you will incur out-of-pocket expenses. For example, if you live in a 3-bedroom townhouse with lease and utilities that cost $1,200 monthly, but the median cost for the dwelling in the area is $1,100 then you have out-of-pocket expenses of $100. The opposite is true for one who chooses to occupy a less expensive residence. Only a member whose housing costs are exactly at or below the median will have no out-of-pocket expenses. BAH is based on civilian standards, considering the housing choices made by civilians of comparable income. Government quarters are assigned based on grade and family size.

Reflection Questions

1) How is my salary determined while I am in the military?

2) What are the benefits of serving 20 years of active-duty in the military?

3) What are some things you should do when talking to a recruiter to ensure that you receive accurate and relevant information?

4) What is the purpose of Basic Training and what are your trainers called while there?

5) Where do you go and what do you do after Basic Training is over?

6) At what point are you officially awarded the title of Soldier, Sailor, Airman, or Marine?

7) What do AIT, MOS, AFSC, and AFSC stand for? Explain each of these acronyms.

8) What percent of individuals who join the military actually make it to the end of their service commitment and either reenlist or walk away content with their Honorable Discharge?

9) What is Basic Housing Allowance and how is it determined?

10) How is BAH distinguished?

Chapter 5
WHAT DOES GOING A.W.O.L. MEAN?

As stated, basic training can be too much for some people to physically and psychologically handle. There are those who lack the physical ability and inner strength to handle the challenges of boot camp and actually go "*Absent Without Leave*" (AWOL) while still at basic training. Basically, AWOL means that a soldier runs away from the military to return to civilian life. Doing this has serious consequences and penalties and sometimes leads to criminal charges. When a soldier is listed as AWOL, the military police are notified and a federal warrant is issued for their arrest. Even months after going AWOL, a soldier can be caught and arrested during a routine traffic stop and then turned over to military authorities. If this happens, or if the soldier surrenders voluntarily, the soldier will be sent back to his or her basic training unit or to Fort Sill for out-processing. Fort Sill is a United States Army post in Lawton, Oklahoma, about 85 miles southwest of Oklahoma City.

Fort Sill is one of the five locations for Army Basic Combat Training. It remains the only active Army installation of all the forts on the South Plains built during the Indian Wars. It is designated as a National Historic Landmark and serves as home of the United States Army Field Artillery School, the Marine Corps' site for Field Artillery MOS school, United States Army Air Defense Artillery School, and is used for training in many other areas.

Consequences of Going AWOL

If a soldier goes AWOL while at basic training, he or she is subject to the same charges and punishments as soldiers who are part of regular units. Going AWOL is covered under Article 86 of the *Uniform Code of Military Justice*, which states that if a soldier:

> *"absents himself or remains absent from his unit, organization, or place of duty at which he is required to be at the time prescribed,"* he or she *"shall be punished as a court-martial may direct."*

The actual application of this law varies and is usually up to the discretion of the company commander. Often the soldier will face nothing more serious than an Article 15, or non-judicial punishment which brings lower pay, confinement to the barracks and extra duty. If a full court-martial results, the soldier will face criminal charges. New recruits who go AWOL usually are expelled from service via an entry-level separation.

Returning to Military Custody After Going AWOL

Out-processing at Fort Sill occurs if the soldier has been dropped from the rolls of a basic-training unit, which happens after 30 days of being declared AWOL. Many people advise AWOL recruits to wait 30 days before turning themselves in if they really want to leave the military, but there is no guarantee that a soldier will be granted an entry-level separation or other favorable discharge. A recruit who surrenders to military authorities as soon as possible after going AWOL shows good faith, has more options and avoids being charged with desertion, an even bigger violation under the *Uniform Code of Military Justice (UCMJ)*.

Alternatives for Discouraged Soldiers

Recruits who are struggling with basic-training have options less drastic than going AWOL. They can seek counsel from a chaplain, medical professional, drill sergeant or company commander. If the soldier still feels he or she cannot cope or is not suited for military life after the fourth week of training, the soldier may request an entry-level separation (ELS). An ELS approval will transfer the soldier to a "holding company" where he or she will wait for the completion of paperwork. It is not uncommon for people to spend weeks at these holding places doing menial labor and waiting.

Organizational Structure

The Department of Defense is headed by the Secretary of Defense, who is a civilian appointed by the President of the United States. Under the Secretary of Defense, there are three military departments: The Department of the Army, the Department of the Navy, and the Department of the Air Force. Each of these military departments are headed by civilians as well. They are: the Secretary of the Army, the Secretary of the Air Force, and the Secretary of the Navy. These service secretaries are also appointed by the President. Below are the four active branches of the military and the position that each of them are headed by:

- The Army is commanded by a four-star general, known as the *Army Chief of Staff* who reports to the Secretary of the Army.

- The Navy is commanded by a four-star admiral, called the *Chief of Naval Operations* who reports to the Secretary of the Navy.

- The top military member in the Air Force is the *Air Force Chief of Staff*. This four-star general reports to the Secretary of the Air Force.

- The Marines is commanded by a four-star general called the *Commander of the Marine Corps* who also reports to the Secretary of the Navy.

These four Flag Officers make up a group called the *Joint Chiefs of Staff (JCS)*. The JCS comprise the four service chiefs, the Vice Chairman of the Joint Chiefs of Staff, and the Chairman of the Joint Chiefs of Staff. The Chairman and the other general and flag officer positions are nominated by the President and approved by the Senate. For operational matters such as war or conflict, the JCS bypasses the individual service secretaries and report directly to the Secretary of Defense and the President.

That leaves the Coast Guard. The Coast Guard does not fall under the Department of Defense. Until recently, the Coast Guard was under the Department of Transportation. Recent legislation has moved the Coast Guard to the newly created Department of Homeland Security. However, the Coast Guard is considered a military service, because, during times of war or conflict, the President of the United States can transfer any or all assets of the Coast Guard to the Department of the Navy. In fact, this has been done in almost every single conflict that the United States has had. The Coast Guard is commanded by a four-star admiral, known as the *Coast Guard Commander*.

Reflection Questions

1) What does AWOL stand for and what does it mean?

2) What happens when a soldier is listed as AWOL?

3) What happens to a soldier when they are returned to military custody after being AWOL for over 30 days?

4) Who heads the Department of Defense and who appoints this person?

5) Who makes up the Joint Chiefs of Staff (JCS) and what do they do?

6) Which branch of the military does not fall under the Department of Defense?

7) What is Fort Sill?

8) How many military departments fall under the Secretary of Defense?

Chapter 6

MILITARY BENEFITS

There are benefits that you and your dependants (if you have any) can enjoy as a result of working for the Federal Government. Every branch of the military offers some form of financial aid to help pay for college. All branches can use the Military Tuition Assistance Program to pay up to 100 percent of college tuition expenses for current military service members. Each branch of the military has its own criteria for eligibility, obligated service time, application process and restrictions. Educational benefits are usually paid directly to the institution by the branch of service you are in. If you want to pursue a higher education, the first thing you must do is check with your military branch to identify specific programs and their eligibility requirements. Most states offer valuable benefits for those who are serving or have served in the armed forces. These benefits include educational grants, scholarships, home loans, veteran's loans, special exemptions or discounts on fees, reduced taxes, free hunting and fishing privileges and more. Each state has and manages their own benefits program for veterans.

The Government Issued (GI) Bill

Getting an education is one of the greatest benefits of serving in the Armed Forces. In 1944, President Franklin D. Roosevelt signed the *Servicemen's Readjustment Act*, otherwise known as the Government Issued (GI) Bill. After World War II, more than two million veterans attended college on the GI Bill. The GI Bill is the centerpiece of the armed service benefits because it encompasses several Department of Veterans Affairs Education Programs including the Post-9/11 GI Bill, The Montgomery GI Bill for Active Duty and Veterans (MGIB-AD), Montgomery GI Bill for Selected Reserves (MGIB-SR), Reserve Education Assistance Program (REAP), Veterans Education Assistance Program (VEAP), Spouse and Dependents Education Assistance (DEA), and the Vocational Rehabilitation and Education (VR&E) Program. This bill provides financial assistance to people who have or are serving in the military for educational and home purchasing purposes. You also may be eligible for more than one educational benefit at a time. Knowing when each is best for your situation can save you money and ensure you get the most out of your benefits.

Congress has given each service the ability to pay up to 100% for the tuition expenses of its members. While in the service, members have access to up to $4,500 a year in Tuition Assistance (as of this writing). Government Issued Bill programs are designed to help active duty, Guard and Reserve service members, and/or veterans and their families earn college degrees, certifications, vocational training or attend trade schools. Depending on the veteran's status, they may receive a monthly benefit which may cover up to 100 percent of their tuition, fees, books and living expenses - all tax-free! The Defense Activity for Non-Tradition Education Support (DANTES) offers service members the opportunity to take college level equivalency exams that can help avoid taking classes in subjects they already know. This saves both time and money while pursuing an education. Armed Forces Tuition Assistance (TA) is a benefit paid to eligible members of the Army, Navy, Air Force, Marines and Coast Guard.

When do the GI Benefits Begin?

To use MGIB while on active duty, you must serve two continuous years of active duty. To use it after honorable separation from active duty, you must have served three continuous years of active duty, unless you were "honorably" discharged early for one of a variety of specific reasons (such as medical). When used after getting out of the military, the G.I. Bill pays more. When used while on active duty, the G.I.

Bill only pays for the cost of tuition for the course. Because of this, most people do not use the G.I. Bill while on active duty, but instead use the military's active duty tuition assistance program. It's important to note that if you are separated early and lose your G.I. Bill qualification, you do not get your money back. This is because under the law, the money taken out of your pay is not considered a "contribution" but rather a "reduction in pay."

Montgomery G. I. Bill for Active Duty

The Active Montgomery GI bill (ADMGIB) is the same for all of the active duty services. The choice of whether or not to participate in the program is up to you, and is made in basic training. This is a **one-time-choice**, and you do not get the chance to change your mind later. If you elect to participate, your military pay is reduced by $100 per month for 12 months ($1,200 total). In return, you receive education benefits worth $37,224 ($30,240 for a two year enlistee). Under the current law, Congress can increase these amounts each year to match inflation. The active duty G.I. Bill benefits can be used while on active duty, or after "honorable" discharge. Benefits expire up to 10 years after discharge. Making the decision is a no-brainer! You will participate in the program if you have any common sense at all. There should be absolutely nothing for you to consider.

Reserve/Guard Montgomery G. I. Bill

Basically, this is the same as the Active Duty Montgomery G. I. Bill, with a few exceptions: The military pay is not reduced for this program. However, your monetary benefits are not nearly as generous as the Active Duty Program. Education benefits for the Guard/Reserve Montgomery G. I. Bill are worth a total of $10,692. You must enlist for a period of six years or more. You can begin using the benefits immediately after boot camp, but benefits terminate if you do not serve your entire enlistment contract period. Benefits expire 14 years after the date you become eligible for the program even if you do not separate.

The Post-9/11 GI-Bill

The Post-9/11 GI Bill provides financial support for education and housing to individuals with at least 90 days of total service on or after September 11, 2001, or individuals discharged with a service-connected disability after 30 days. You must have received an honorable discharge to be eligible for the Post-9/11 GI Bill. As of August 1, 2009, the Post-9/11 GI Bill is effective for training also. Approved training under the Post-9/11 GI Bill includes graduate, undergraduate degrees, and vocational/technical training. All training programs must be offered by an institution of higher learning and approved for GI Bill benefits. Tutorial assistance, licensing and certification test reimbursement are also approved under the Post- 9/11 GI Bill.

The Post-9/11 GI Bill will pay tuition based upon the highest in-state tuition charged by a public educational institution in the state where the school is located. The amount of support that an individual may qualify for depends on where they live and what type of degree they are pursuing. For more expensive tuition, a program exists which may help to reimburse the difference. This program is called the "Yellow Ribbon Program". The Post 9-11 GI Bill will pay the following to eligible individuals:

- Tuition and fees directly to the school not to exceed the maximum in-state tuition and fees at a public Institution of Higher Learning

- A monthly housing allowance based on the basic allowance for housing for an E-5 with dependents at the location of the school

- An annual books and supplies stipend of $1,000 paid proportionately based on enrollment

- A one-time rural benefit payment for eligible individuals

The benefits under this bill are payable only for training at Institutions of Higher Learning. If you are enrolled exclusively in online training, you will not receive the housing allowance. If you are on active duty you will not receive the housing allowance or books and supplies stipend. This benefit provides up to 36 months of education benefits. Generally benefits are payable for 15 years following release from active duty. The Post-9/11 GI Bill also offers some service members the opportunity to transfer their GI Bill to their dependents. If you are eligible and depending on program imposed limits, the Veteran's Association (VA) will pay your tuition portion directly to the school. These limits are the most expensive in-state public college undergraduate tuition in your school's state multiplied by your entitlement percentage (calculated by number of months served on active duty since September).

As has been stated several times throughout this book, you must know that joining the military is absolutely what you want to do. Serving can be a very fulfilling and rewarding experience and will make you a different and better person. Those who decide to go into the military right after high school as opposed to going to college right after, can get the experience of Armed Forces Training and then use the military benefits to pay for college afterwards. Some may see this as the better of two worlds. There is great pride in serving in the military and those who risk their lives for the freedom of America are highly esteemed and greatly honored. In a nutshell, the benefits of joining the U.S. Armed forces are great, but the sacrifice and pride of being a U.S. Armed Services hero can be even greater. Below are the main benefits that service men/women receive as a member of the U.S. Armed Forces:

Steady Income: You are generally paid on the 1st and 15th of every month, based on your pay grade and service requirements.

Advancement: You are promoted based on your job knowledge, your performance and your time in pay grade and service requirements.

Paid vacation: You earn 2.5 days paid vacation per month for a total of 30 days each year up to 60 days.

Training: You choose your career path based on your aptitude, physical abilities, security clearance, motivation and determination. All specialties are open to women, including combat roles.

Health Care: While on active duty, you will receive complete medical and dental care at no cost to you.

Life Insurance: Active duty members select up to $200,000 in term life insurance for only $18 per month.

Allowances: You may also receive additional tax-free money for basic allowance Housing (BAH) if government housing is not available; Basic Allowance for Subsistence (BAS), if government food facilities are not available in the area you are stationed; and a uniform allowance (for enlisted personnel only) to help you maintain your uniform.

Tax Advantage: Only your basic monthly pay is subject to Federal or State income tax.

GI Bill: The Montgomery GI Bill will help pay for college education or vocational training.

Tuition Assistance: While on active duty, you may continue your education and may be assistance in defraying the cost of college-accredited courses.

Additional Benefits: There are exchange and commissary privileges, moving allowances, temporary lodging expenses, travel, survivor benefits, Veterans Administration benefits home loans and more.

Reflection Questions

1) In your own words, explain the GI Bill.

2) What are the benefits of the GI bill?

3) How many years must you serve in active duty in order to use the the Montgomery GI Bill?

4) Which bill provides financial support for education and housing to individuals with at least 90 days of total service on or after September 11, 2001, or individuals discharged with a service-connected disability after 30 days.

5) When do you make the decision of taking advantage of the GI Bill and how does this affect your pay?

6) When can you start benefiting from the MGIB?

7) If you are separated early or lose your GI Bill qualification, do you get your money back? Explain.

8) Explain the Yellow Ribbon Program.

FREQUENTLY ASKED QUESTIONS ABOUT THE U.S. ARMED FORCES

1. **How do I know which branch to join?**
   You must decide which branch is the better fit for you based upon your interests, skills, and abilities. Each of the armed services are different, and some may be more suited for one branch over another. Be sure that you select a branch that you are interested in joining based upon *your* interests and not because of someone else's interests.

2. **What if I don't make a high score on the ASVAB?**
   If you barely meet the qualifying test score, then rest assured that you will not have a large variety of jobs from which to choose. If you score too low, you will not qualify to join the military.

3. **How long will I have to serve in the military?**
   When you make the decision to join the military whether it is for a part time or full time basis, you commit yourself for a minimum of eight years.

4. **How old do I have to be to join the military?**
   You can join the military at 17 years of age with your parent's permission.

5. **If I am not an American citizen can I join the military?**
   Only U.S. citizens or foreign nationals legally residing in the United States with an Immigration and Naturalization Service Alien Registration Card (Green Card - INS Form I-151/551) may apply. Applicants must speak, write and read English fluently.

6. **What are the benefits of joining the military?**
   The benefits are many, but the main ones are:
   - Steady Income
   - Advancement opportunities
   - Paid vacation
   - Training
   - Health Care
   - Life Insurance
   - Allowances
   - Tax Advantage
   - GI Bill benefits
   - Tuition Assistance
   - Additional Benefits

7. **Can I go to college while I'm in the military?**
   You can use the MGIB while on active duty after you have served two continuous years of active duty.

8. **How long is Basic Training?**
   Basic Training can range anywhere from six to thirteen weeks.

9. **What is the purpose of Basic Training?**
   Basic Training or Military "Boot Camp" is six to thirteen weeks of extremely intense physical military training and teaches warfighting skills.

   It is the job of the Training Instructors (TIs) and Drill Instructors (DIs) to either alter your mind-set to a military way of thinking or weed you out before the military spends too much money on your training. This is done by applying extreme degrees of physical and mental strain while simultaneously teaching you the essentials of military rules, policies, protocol, and the logistics of your particular branch of service.

10. **Will I have to pay for food and shelter in the military?**
 No, all of your food and shelter is paid for in the military.

11. **Can I choose to be based at a location close to home?**
 You probably would have little to no say in what your first duty station is. Your first duty station would last about two to three years. After that, you may make a request, but there is no guarantee that you will get it.

12. **How intense is the Physical Training?**
 Each service branch has a different series of physical requirements, but the most common among each branch are the sit-ups, push-ups, pull-ups, endurance run and swim.

13. **What if I don't pass the Physical Training?**
 If you fail the physical aspect of basic training, drill sergeants will work with you, and you will be retested after about 90 days; but if you fail a second time, then your chances of moving forward in the military are very slim.

14. **Which medical conditions will disqualify me from joining the military?**
There is a list of medical conditions that will not allow you to join if you suffer from them. A recruiter can review the list with you.

15. **Will I have to go to Iraq or Afghanistan if I join the military?**
You will not automatically be sent to Iraq or Afghanistan right away. When you finish your job training, you will report to your first duty station. If your new unit is getting set to deploy, then you will go with them. Units are usually told about 6-10 months in advance about upcoming deployments, but they are not locked into it until about three months beforehand. However, there is always a chance that the unit you get assigned to is deploying 2 weeks after you get there, and if that is the case, then yes, you must go with them.

16. **Will I use a gun in the military?**
Not everyone uses a gun in the military. It depends upon what your job is and what you have trained for.

17. **How often will I be able to come home?**
You earn 2.5 days a month, which equates to 30 days of vacation a year to do as you please.

18. **Do they have military sports teams?**
Yes. The Armed Forces Sports (AFS) makes it possible for military personnel to have the opportunity to train and compete for national, Olympic and international competitions, such as the International Military Sports Council (CISM) and the World Military Championships. The AFS program is the culmination of each branch of Services' sports and fitness program. Service members participate and compete at unit level intramurals and advance to the All-Service level. The AFS continues to provide an avenue for military Service members to participate in national and international competitions.

The sports offered through this program include boxing, cross country (M/W), women's basketball, beach volleyball, bowling, women's soccer, indoor volleyball (M/W), triathlon, rugby, softball (M/W), golf (M/W), marathon (M/W), men's basketball, men's soccer

19. **Will I be able to get a good job when I come out of the military?**
Absolutely! Many of the skills that you learn in the military can be carried over into civilian life.

FACTS ABOUT THE MILITARY

- ✓ When you make the decision to join the military whether it is a on a part time or full times basis, you commit yourself for a minimum of eight years.

- ✓ The Commander and Chief of the American Military is the President of the United States.

- ✓ The score you get on the ASVAB will determine the type of job you will train for in the military.

- ✓ If you score too low on the ASVAB, you will not qualify to join the military.

- ✓ You must do the best you can on the ASVAB so that you will be eligible for the job that matches your ability and interests.

- ✓ There are nine enlisted ranks in the military.

- ✓ There are no doctors, nurses, or enlisted medics in the Marine Corps.

- ✓ There is no Marine Corps National Guard.

- ✓ The President of the United States can transfer part or all of the Coast Guard to the Department of the Navy in times of conflict.

- ✓ Legislation that was passed in 2002 transferred the Coast Guard to the Department of Homeland Security.

- ✓ All of the services have a reserve component and two of the services (Army and Air Force) have a National Guard.

- ✓ The primary purpose of the Reserves and National Guard is to provide a reserve force to supplement the active duty forces when needed.

- ✓ State governors can call out their National Guard units to assist in state emergencies.

- ✓ The Army is the agency that organizes and trains soldiers for land warfare.

- ✓ The main purpose of the Army is to protect and defend the United States by way of ground troops, armor tanks, artillery, attack helicopters, tactical nuclear weapons, etc.

- ✓ The Army is supported by two Reserve Forces: The Army Reserves and the Army National Guard.

- ✓ The primary difference between the Reserves and the National Guard is that the Reserves are owned and managed by the federal government and the National Guard is owned by individual states.

- ✓ The President of the United States or the Secretary of Defense can activate National Guard members into Federal Military Service during times of need.

- ✓ The Navy's primary mission is to maintain "freedom of the seas."

- ✓ In times of conflict, the Navy helps to supplement Air Force air power. The Navy is also responsible for transporting Marines to areas of conflict.

- ✓ Unlike the Army and Air Force, there is no Naval National Guard (although a few states have established "Naval Militias").

- ✓ The Air Force is the youngest military service.

- ✓ The Marines do not mix men and women in basic training.

- ✓ The primary duty of the Marines is to assault, capture, and control "beach heads" which is a position on an enemy

- ✓ shoreline captured by troops in advance of an invading force.

- ✓ The Marines are often referred to as the *"Infantry of the Navy."*

- ✓ There is no Marine Corps National Guard.

- ✓ During times of peace, the Coast Guard is primarily concerned with law enforcement, boating safety, sea rescue, and illegal immigration control.

- ✓ Much of what you are going to experience in Basic Training can be practiced at home before you even go off to Basic Training.

- ✓ When going into the military, it is to your advantage to prepare yourself to be rigorously challenged mentally and physically.

- ✓ Each service branch has a different series of physical requirements, but the most common among each branch are the sit-ups, push-ups, pull-ups, endurance run and swim.

- ✓ The purpose of DOD medical standards is to ensure that medically qualified personnel are accepted into the Armed Forces of the United States.

- ✓ Lying to get into the military is punishable by a $10,000 fine and/or three years in prison!

- ✓ The GI Bill is the centerpiece of the Armed Service benefits because it encompasses several Department of Veterans Affairs Education Programs.

- ✓ The Defense Activity for Non-Tradition Education Support (DANTES) offers service members the opportunity to take college level equivalency exams that can help avoid taking classes in subjects they already know.

- ✓ To use MGIB while on active duty, you must serve two continuous years of active duty.

- ✓ If you are separated early and lose your G.I. Bill qualification, you do not get your money back.

- ✓ The choice of whether or not to participate in education the program is up to you. The decision is made in basic training. It is a **one-time-choice**, and you do not get the chance to change your mind later.

About the Author

Dr Mia Y. Merritt was born and raised in Miami Florida and matriculated in the Miami-Dade County Public School System. She is an educator with over 17 years experience working as a teacher, Assistant Principal, College Professor and mentor. She is a Certified Keynote Speaker, Teen/Youth Facilitator, Radio Talk Show Host, Prosperity Coach and Author.

Dr. Merritt has provided workshops, seminars and keynote speeches around the country to organizations such as the U.S. Department of Homeland Security, The Miami-Dade County City Mangers, FIU Executive Staff, University of Miami Public Relations Department, Family Christian Association and many more.

She holds a Bachelors Degree in Elementary Education, a Masters Degree in Exceptional Education, a Specialist Degree in Educational Leadership and a Doctorate Degree in Organizational Leadership.

Dr. Merritt is a published author of fourteen books on the subjects of spirituality, personal development, prosperity, self-empowerment, and adult education.

To purchase 'All About the Military' please contact
1-866-560-7652

Discounts are available for bulk purchases.

This book and others on similar subjects may be found at www.amazon.com or www.barnesandnoble.com under the author Mia Merritt.

www.ingramcontent.com/pod-product-compliance
Lightning Source LLC
Chambersburg PA
CBHW031209090426
42736CB00009B/850